A World of Fairies
in Grayscale
Coloring Book for Adults

Illustrated by Molly Harrison

www.mollyharrisonart.com

Molly Harrison 10/08

Molly Harrison 12-31-07

Molly Harrison 12/1

Molly Harrison 12/2007

Molly Harrison 3/07

Molly Harrison 2007

Molly Harrison
2/13

Molly Harrison 9-06

Molly Harrison 2011

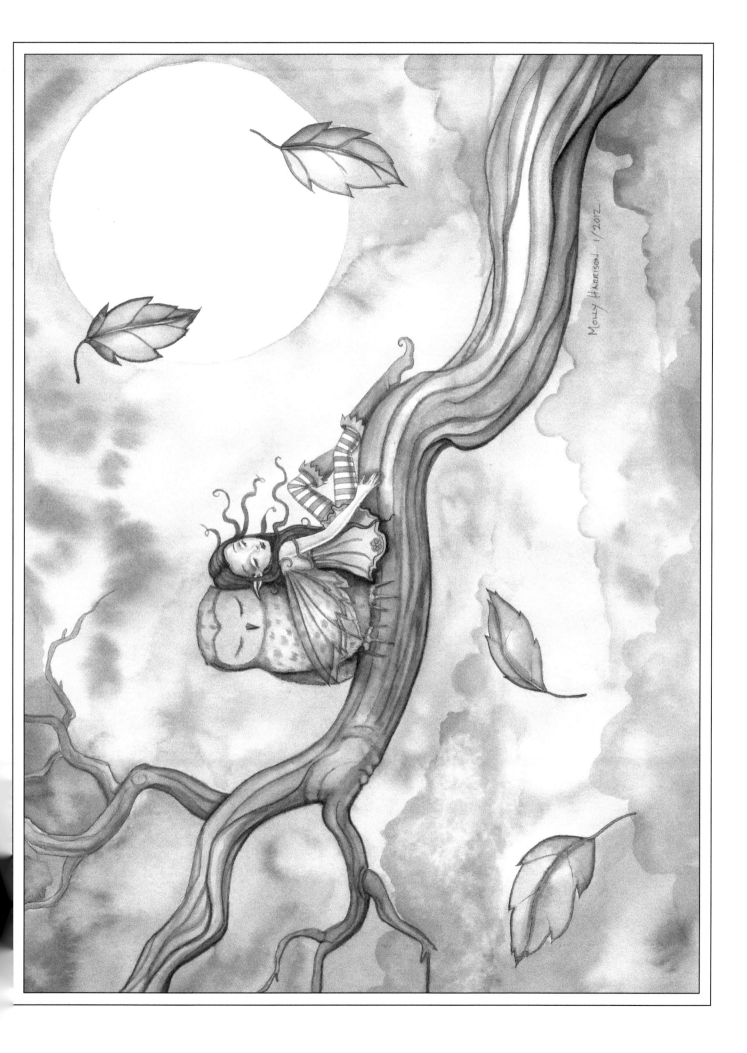

Molly Harrison 2011

Molly Harrison
4/09

Thank you for purchasing this coloring book!

Please see Molly's website, The Fantasy Art of
Molly Harrison, www.mollyharrisonart.com for
digital, printable PDFs of these coloring books as
well as individual coloring pages!

Other books include:

Enchanted Sea (Grayscale)
Fairyland
Fantasy Art Coloring Book
Mermaid Coloring Book
Maigical Fairies of Molly Harrison
Unicorns and Dragons (with fairies)
Fairies and Fantasy
Halloween Coloring Book
Holiday Coloring Fun
Mystical
Autumn Fantasy
Autumn Magic (Grayscale)
Whimsical World
Whimsical World #2
Whimsical Halloween
Whimsical Winter Wonderland
Fairy Coloring Book (Grayscale)
Fairies and Mermaids (Grayscale)
Bohemian Fantasy (Grayscale)
Colorful Fantasy;

Molly Harrison is an artist working out of her home studio in northern
California. Molly works primarily in watercolor and ink bringing you
fairies, fantasy art, wildlife art, and more! Please visit The Fantasy Art
of Molly Harrison, www.mollyharrisonart.com for more information.
You can find Molly's prints on her website and Etsy.

CPSIA information can be obtained
at www.ICGtesting.com
Printed in the USA
LVHW052357281018
595076LV00004B/34/P

9 781542 640985